The True
Sea of Life

Robert Nathaniel Oriyama'at

www.lulu.com
If you have any questions
Email me @

Rob7_o@yahoo.com

First Edition:
2008 by Robert Nathaniel Oriyama'at(paperback)

All rights reserved. No part of this book may be reproduced,in whole or in part, in any form or by any means, electronic or mechanical, including photocopying, recording, or by any information storage and retrieval system without the constent publisher. No part of this book may be reproduce without permission in writing from the publisher. Inquiries should be addressed to Rob7_o@yahoo.com www.myspace.com/absoluteconnsciencepharaohe

© Library of Congress Catalog Card Number:
ISBN 978-0-615-25766-2(paperback)
Printed in the United States of America

-

-

THIS POETRY IS DEDICATED TO: ALLAH/GOD, Master Fard Muhammad, My dad,my sister Jennifer.My half sister Roberta.(Keep doing you) Aja-Monet, I don't know you much, but to just to see you perform for the first time in the Nuyorican Cafe gave me more encouragement to become a poet. Second is Khemraf, who had inspired me to become a poet, when he told me that three years ago. I hadn't listened then, but now I'm moving forward with it. Minister Farrakhan,(one of my mentors), Fidel Castro,(my other mentor), Hugo Chavez, The U.S. government. (The good and the bad of it, I still love this government)My little sister Calonie, (you are a great artist), I love you. Let the light shine on you, so you can shine yourself.) My best friend Kenneth Pugh and Lawda Pugh, (I love ya, wherever yous are.) Denise Aguilar from Brockton, Mass (I'm in Boston, call me).Sabrina Todd,(thanks for the friendship we had. I miss you.) My friend Jason (Half-Italian, Half-Panamanian) Flaco Nunez(Gracias pa' la mensaje), Orishas(Queda haciendo la cosa tuya.) Telmary and Yusa, Sergio Mendes, Silvio Rodriquez, Prince, Nas, Jedi Mind Tricks, Michael Jackson, George Clinton, Bro Sunni from the BX, Bro. Minister Tony from YO, Bro Minister Arthur,(I miss yall so much, you just don't know) Bro Elijah Shabazz, Bro Captain Dennis, (Bpt) Supreme Captain Mustapha, Bro James 30x, Bro Robert 18X, Bro Hakim(Whats Happening?, Love), Bro Henry. Shabazz from Bridgeport, Kevin Sabio,(Somos Venceremos!!!!)Twice Thou, (I love you, brother, New England for life.) Ray Benzino (Boston, Holla back!) Tego Calderon, (You like my dad, gave me pride to be Afro-Latin, Te amo pana) Intifada, Cuz Tayron, Tasha, Ferdina,Tessi, Phyllis, Aunt Betty, Uncle Sonny, Aunt Martha.Aunt Fannie, My favorite Cuz Thamas (I miss you so much) My cuz Terrance y Tyler, Ebony(I'm going to eat your food) Teresa y Rob, my friend Gary y saborcita Cathy, Terrell, Jovan, my sister Roberta,(Big brother got love for ya) My uncle J.C. My uncle Herc, Aunt Bessie, All of my Afro Latinos, West Indians, and Afro Americans, Cape Verde, My God-father Tony Lazarus, All of the Latin America, the world, All the poets, my lawyer Ed Paquette. Jeremy Joyce(I love you you saved my life.) Jennifer Caban, The Caban Family, Mexican Del Rio Melissa, who was adopted (I wish I knew before, I love you, I'll never forget you) My friend Torri' , Pat, Haitian Mike Corelone(Air force) Q Vo from East L.A., Del Rio, TX, San Antonio, TX , Cuidad Acuna, Eagle Pass, Piedras Negras, Bonnie. (I miss you) Houston, TX, New Orleans, LA, South Korea, New Jersey, Terp from the BRICKS!!!!!!!!!!!!!!! The Bryant family.(I love yall) Forty from Prince Street Projects, (Real Street Dude, you in TX, But I know you holding Jerz, down. Philly, DJ Volton from the BX (We doing big things fam) , Power 99, Visunique, T-Rock, D.C. My fam from B-more. NI CEEEEEEEEEEEEEEEEEEE and CONNNNNNNNNNIIEEE, Aunt Bernice, and Uncle Willie,(Da Mets?) Now to New York, BROOKLYN!!!!! Bedstuy,Greene Ave, Fulton St, Bro Jabril, (Respect for Life black man. We got this world open) Da Guru.(I'm staying up with you brother) Catlin Messiner, (You from Bedstuy) Alterego, Tantra, TONE, from Bushwick, Buckshot, Smif n Wesson,Evelyn, Dana, Dawn,and Falon , Brother Homer, two many to name from Brooklyn....I love yall that showed me love when I was there. Manhattan, Taino Towers, Sister with the hair product. UPACA, Lexington Ave 116th street, 125th street. LES, Nuyorican Cafe, (Love it!!!!!!!!!) Bowery Cafe,(Haven't hit that yet) The BX all day, 2917 Grand Concourse Bldg. 199th street posse., Queens, Jamacia, south side, Quesha, Wilford,Willie Cheryl, Cuban Prince, Ipphiphany, (You are gorgeous!!) Quesha's cuz from Ocean Ave, East NY. Denisha, my family in Long Island, Hempstead, Freeport, etc. Love to ALLLLLLLL!

Hope you love what I have to offer

Working in spiritually in these last days of time.

    Origin....
    The God in Me
    Abraham
    Mi Consciencia
    Chains will be broken
    The God in me, Part II

New England Times (The New England State of Mind)

    New England life (Hell's womb, Womb of America)
    Providence
    Boston......Beantown mashing.
    Bridgeport, Da Port of Envy
    Bridgeport, Da Port of Envy Part II
    New England Underworldz
    When the God speaks

Viwws of hope to master trials with errors

    Liberalism
    Ojala
    Trial with Errors

Dwelling on the Omen on our actions

    Difficult History
    Courage to Change
    Wrath of the Math
    Wake from Bilal

The struggle of my Humanity

    My humanity
    Quiere me como soy

Words of Concern of the Nation

    Last of the dying breed

Love in the end

    Re.....wind

Working in spiritually in these last days of time

Origin......

This was a poem to a woman that I admire with curiousity....

Originality is something that comes from the self

and what we see in the world

is just otherwise.

sad thing to see

but I know that the meaning of the originality

second coming of change

change only come to love life

Love

what is love?

People know but

most interpret on greed and lust

Impatience is the biggest problem

For God had mercy on us

We fools

We lust for the external

The elements are not interpretive to the eye or mind

waste of time

I get annoyed on waste

Imperfection comes from not being patient

in seeing that we are the option

as God is

Why does he exist then?

We fools,

Anger can be change to happiness

I do not expect to see all change

I know the nature of things to bring about change

though I fear not to bring in congruence

parallel to what I was given from God

I'm grateful

But what about the people

if you lose all money,

you lose all faith?

Mary is the womb

Abraham is the way

A child yearning to learn must be born

Why be in a box?

A trend and not trendsending

you spoke the same

I know for some time in thought

A thought

A response is a reaction to intrepret

from now we being original

That is why it will work

The God in me

Rite where you stand,
slap jaw you, your fork tongue bleeding
I smite that bow out your hand
Damn those who out to assasinate
the ones who out to display the band
of Abraham,
like gamma rays, to cancer man
destroy with lucumi con dios
arroz con habichuelos
no embrollos(Confusion)
with character killing fellows
when thinking our shit is sweet
when in top secret now
we hard to defeat,
like overwhelming gravity
to flame blower with mental cavity
wishing to burn me
gradually I origin again
like scalping heads
possessing your foul unit
and staging it above the rim
here coming the arrows of sour and sweet
13 of them mastering the sin
Cere bums

lost the war

time and time is in

wasted like Marilyn Mason

I'm the best when

Pondering skull and bones with gin

try to break my pyriprism

In elevated places

immunity from iniquity, the mission

myself fade out with humbleness

but stern to rebuke

transgressionism jugarism con exorcism

no kin

in my circumference

cause I'm immense with indualities

that's random

playing to win over sinscience fatalites

and tynegod, is I fighting to win

I may die for what I love

Z ONE IN

always observing the enemiticious

thinking pattern too stale to me

I been fictious

and now my mind is black like licorice.

Abraham

Blessed to all people who out to make a difference.

Days and days

go by like the Protocols of Satan

into even the lost found people

we still are that, why some think

that you are free from complete revolution?

Be optimistic on your life.

Being saved is nonsense.

This world is bold to practice tongue with no clarity

no action like an M-16 in a foxhole guarding your gate.

nor requisitioning of loyalty, like tails of F15E

by sourcing closest to your soul,

Maybe because we ran away like Jonah.

and the Deutoronomy had us with frost bites on our souls

and our minds are in phases,

Like the phases of Betelgueuse

That big red star, don't even think it still exist

light years are actually heavy

That dying world we are in

the illusion it is, but yet we don't know

We don't calculate, because we don't practice the order

At least try, No fear.

Like Soju at Pyongtek

Ready to lose worthless matter?

But I don't need no more to quote names out that are worthy

Because I myself out to practice Abraham

Or Ibrahim, like Ferrer(PBUH)

Or like Garveyism.

See I didn't suppose to quote

I start my own Ori and dwell with the thoughts that travel 24,000,000 miles per sec.

and destined to find every square inch of circumference of history...

within

that starts with the number 24

24,896 square miles in circumference

24 elders of master of : Circle, square, tri-angle

into format.

Be Abraham

That you can go through Rocky IV training

and the tongues of hammers

to mash out indirect or direct dogma

Be Abraham

So you can be blessed with seeds.

Never stick your hand in planted ones

Be Abraham so you live to be 1000

That is a 1000 times likely to burn calories

that the brain can be free to posses more data

that sticks to you like a virgin gottenbe with pinga

That way your brain cell can start a juicy shischabob.

So much water like rain drops with waterlets

atoms combined makes more time

and shine energy, free of cost

and now who's the boss?

Faith like the dove came after the triumph of Old Cuba.

Take a knive and cut your lust, hate, envy, and jealousy

and not at the alter

but only with ego

Triumvirate and you're a Caesar

with the compass that God gave (Genesis 15:13)

But the fallen angel stopped in your mist of consciousness

Mi consciencia

Mi consciencia es como fuego

que no puede poner fuera

como Tego

porque mi pecho es en la derecha manera

Sera' en la cima de las montanas de Israel

Con la verdad

Que lo que sera'

No me gusta la gente que estan diciendo mierda

La mierda no pasa conmigo

Cuando yo estoy frustrado, se iba al biblio y coran para panera

La mentirmierda, avisaronlo, sobre nuestra cultura es hispano todo

Nuestra gente que sigue' , esta loco

Loco porque ellos han perdieron suyos almas

en las manos de la gente se llama Zionistas

y las illuminatistas, pero ni tampoco

Sunoco, ellos tienen con no negocio

con cortesia con los otros

Los otros son nosotros

que tienen las almas se roto

porque de esclavidad pa' los siglos

Es peligro

De los colores hermosos diferentes de nosotros

negro, marron, rojo, amarillo, a casi blanco

en que asistimos en este Estato con odio

pa' el color otro, ademas que somos famila

pero no tranquila, no alegria,

como eso, nuestra alma, no tenia.

Naranjito estoy diciendo

Mi piel es lejo de negro

Pero como tego

Con oscuridad, llego

con fuego

Porque mi consciencia es como fuego.

Chains Will Be Broken

Will be broken..
is the chain of being subjugated
by mental psychics of lust of power,
heart broken women,
I now do feel your pain,
the envious with hatred,
and my anxiety to see peace at last in all my struggle
I now live with the sense of freedom
a sense of better understanding and expression of my will
Material things that I possess will not.
It is the freedom to express my piece of mind
regardless of what people think of me
cause they are transgressors, causing to trample my will
the ones who are there are few, but that is enough
Khemraf, you inspired me in many ways to advance
My mexicana amiga Mary, Nunca olividate, nunca
to the goldiggers and the other women that try to control me
and break me down to make me less of a man
you made me sharper
cause my heart is too strong
Death before dishonor, those now read this to just after
have negative thoughts in their sick minds
for you and yours, the sowing of the wrath

of my positive spirit that travels

like Orishas to the jiniteros

to the Huey Newtons, and Clayton Powells

HabanaNueva, (New Haven) I love my Cuban culture

there are those out to whiten my culture and make it like

we are bunch of ignorant street man.

For they want to stop the moment of a strong young black man

like me, who don't tolerate foolishness, and mentiras,

I speak none of. Thanks to Alterego to express her mind

and others who do so. There is no need to be fixed

for the thinking pattern you make out,

not be fixed by opinonated missionaries

avisaron on lies and theories

and some who speak on freedoms

still reap on some of what I say

I don't just support the revolution, I am one revolution

The Question is?

What is revolution....I know what it is....don't judge me

Judge yourself....you walk your shoes...

so look at the bottom.

Is the foundation sturdy like iron?

or soft as clay?

May God give us wisdom like Jose Marti

plus Tupac had wisdom

Stop judging other things of his character

That is the problem that we keep adding

to the vortex, that we all victim of

No Mentira(No lies) We had enuff.

I see now where my destiny can be

if I stay strong...I will speak to millions

and sometimes just hundreds like before

I have great wisdom...It is God's wisdom

My wife will be the same..

No lie, I don't like transgressors,

She will respect me of who I am

and I will respect her the same

My children will live to see the truth

and no brainwashed americanized

way of life. I pray on Africa, China, the Far East

the Palestinians and Latin America

become more in control of their will and destiny

of the guajiros, the African and Indian Diaspora

I love Hugo Chavez as well as Fidel Alejandro Castro Ruz.

Born in Biran, Cuba Of a wealthy white spanish man

and black woman of Cuba..

I never forgive those that killed The Argentinan brother

Ernesto "Che" Guevara.

I am not afraid to speak the truth.

on how they did many others.

Don't read this and judge my character..

Cause you don't no me..and will just know me

of my book and speeches...

God bless the children who hold their own.

New England Times(The New England State of Mind)

New England Life (Hell's womb, Womb of America)

Yeah right

New England life

sounds nice

can be definitently

But at a costly Price

Without da doe

Crackin yeyo in da cold

will be yo nightlife

Hell with that postcard shit

Outsidaz will get the vibes right

Unless you got doe off da ying yang

You see yourself in Greenwich, Nantucket

or New Canaan

Cause you seeing more green than Boston Common

Otherwise your just getting by

Slangin

Or totin toast threatening bang bang

Everywhere in Southern New England

Same thang

For some outsidaz that sounds strange

But New England is the whole model

of this whole game

Dont know too much about

Vermont, New Hampshire or Maine

But Connecticut, Massachussetts, and Rhode Island

Be ready like da MinuteMan

before retirin

for dat doe

Here many broads be lyin

I'm like Tom Brady seein a TD

Passing

Firin'

The best haters here

cryin

cause they can't see me

like whale watch on TV

Tax brokers be after me

wanting my pockets empty

like these factories

I still seeing

Cape Cod

sippin non-alcholic dacgery

smokin out stress

like ED. OG

Be I downlow

MC

Da frontin Industry

Acting like I a new jack

That's how it be's

when outsidaz see

us latino and blacks.

Ain't shit sweet

Crosstown beef

Where's Uncle Sam's police

Theres beef even between streets

Huh?

Thats da plan though

to leave us 6 feet deep

Hell with dat

I'm still was trying to eat

Even now

Ends justifies the means

to make sure they meet

like old Whalers Bruins games

running back

like Graig James

the history

The ghosts of New England

still a mystery

give back the Constitution to Connecticut

don't throw it out

cause corruption is hell it gets

from equal opportunity

Politicans faking people unity

Many of us on bracelets

Social economical whip

here the biggest

Most of our cities

need total facelifts

Most Manufacturing jobs left

already long before the first Asics

like loose laces

been tripped up

like Larry Bird's mind

with the Pacers

with Isiah

Here many rhymsayers

but can't shine like real players

cause the coaches made A/Rs

to us the big haters

Cause of politics practical

Secret like Skull n Bones

a mason

Mas on , Build on

infiltrate us lab rats

with trends

the spirit of the American way

Like Malcolm, MLK and Louis Farakhan

studied the trends to spurge to other states later

Us not nationally known as rhymesayers

Cause in New England

the past and the present of trend

can make us rhyme greater

Providence

From a young seed

The last months of a dyin breed

Me not knowin

You placed me in the world full with dis ease

Sins of inquities

Where exactly in Hell's Kitchen

New England, my Lord The Mighty

In Bridgeport, Connecticut

I was just a kid

in the Bloody Bridge

despite seein' and hearin'

people dyin', my heart was cryin'

Still you let me live

But before

It seemed many times you have closed the door

Seein' my father clingin' the knife at my mother

Wait, there's more

Seein' at Father Panik Village, wilding brothers

at 49 Brick Buildings,

4 stories high, brothers chillin' like a villain.

Straight gutta

One way in , with speed bumps now

One way out the otha

Lord, I'm sure

I saw was war

You showed what I had to bore

I was quiet

Observing the tour

On Stratford Ave

Seeing Prostitutes

Another word for whores

Yes I had my part

doing some dirt in the start

But

My mother for 2 years

had me in catholic school

In New England

The Industrial Revolution and the best Institutions ruled

New York City was just the heart

Satan's world at the womb

Smokestacks, liquor stores, the society secret

deception to the tomb

I desire for life to the fullest

merging from doom

Why we don't understand?

Our mothers and fathers

Died from us, so soon.

My mother was a witness

Supposely from Jehovah

She showed me the bible

meaning book, Never forget this

Basic/Instructions/Before/Leaving/Earth

I love my mother, but she ain't with this

My pops was 13

After my Cuban abuelo died, spiri was in bricklist

Is it our fault, Lord?

That we have to go through so much

smokin' reefer

gettin' dust

abusin' our women

because of Lust?

What!

Yes, Jesus

Christ, meaning anointed

Civilized people, to the cross to save us.

Why was he anointed to go through so much pain?

Besides havin universal and Earthly laws in his brain?

Lord, was that what the Golden bar mean't?

Only to die for us FOOLISH people livin in vain?

The whippings and beatings physically
of the son of man, lingage of kings

The brainwashing of opinions, theories,illusions

Is all the same

The fact that in time periods that hanged

We was reduced to foolishness

The reason the anointed one came

Lord, Jehovah

They came for what?

We don't understand the reason

To fulfill Yahweh, (yah way) in English version

with righteousness, not treason

Genesis 1:26, yah way in image and in likeness

Who is yah?

The father, son, and holy spirit,

saved in one man

No flaw

was in Adam until....

Why these Politicans still?

Got us trapped in hell?

Mayor Ganim, and Mayor Cianci in the cell

Got us New Englanders ringin' bells

We all knowing

We're like lab rats under the rug

Live, but can't tell

Hip hop, into rap

Refining into blinding

Still Hip Hop in New England

ain't Shinin'

Like it is all sweet

Armaggedeon turf wars

Crosstown beef

President Bush?

Why God Why?

Did you let him be chief?

Providence

The meaning of it we all should seek.

Nostradamus said of the 4 comings

Of what?

Jesus, the son of man

Nostradamus, the Jewish scholar,

was right about the two twins

Why God, we stay so weak?

Astray from your Glory

Desire and will

Our word we must keep

To the death like "Che" Guevara

Self made doctor

Checkmate with Jesus, we must meet

Providence

The meaning of it we all should seek

But God , This is Satan's system.

Mom and Dad, no trust

Please have mercy on our women

They're victims

They fed us

Clothed us

They got our women on some mission

Loyalty

Can be life and death

Love is what I'm missing

Seems like there is no where to turn

Where is the Second coming of the Son of Man fishing?

Son Of Man

What is the definition?

Somebody tell me before the Great Day.

I know Satan is listening

What Government holds such Constitution

of the Gateway State?

But it just solidifies their abusin.

illusions.

Minds in fantasy cruising.

Cities are dead

from Bridgeport to Fall River

Mill Rate is high

The drug flow, low in deliver

Bridgeport #1

Providence#4 in property tax, having you shiver.

Cycles

Trends begin to quiver society

Full Capitalism

at this peak

Why God Why?

Wheres Jesus

I seek

Providence

The meaning of it we all should seek.

Shout out to Tanisha, Paris, and his wife and the other people I met in Providence

This poem was done about three years ago. I went to Providence Rhode Island at one time at Indian Point at the Cape Verdean Festival. It was beautiful. One of my cousins and I went to the place and heard about it from a friend who was a former Brown Univ

Coach. The scenery was beautiful. A girl named Tanisha, who was actually Cape Verdean also had invited us to go to this poetry session in Providence. So this was done there. This was officially was my second poetry done period. My first was an Controversal poetry done in Muhammad's Mosque #7 in New York where I used to be in the ranks in the Nation of Islam. The reason I said it was controversial because the most people in the ranks wasn't ready to accept the poem. Because many people in the Mosque ain't ready to accept the Teachings of Elijah Muhammad. These teachings is for all of humanity to prosper. But we, who are the children of Israel(The supplanter) are ready as a group to proceed to building a Nation so whe no long be a child of Israel. We would be on the mountains of Israel. Most of us in general do things because of emotions and we let ourselves to be consumed by these emotions. Therefore we are stagnate. We still are beneficaries of the government of the United States. A country that has a debt of over 450 billion dollars owed to various countries and China is number one on the list.

Boston ....Beantown mashing!!!!!!

I'm out in the Bean, getting the Hub in smash
like soon smashing a beat by Ap
on the New England set
now a Massachussetts resident
from catching politican corruption prone Connecticut
A Bridgeport soldier
A Number 1 draft pick
Gunzout Entertainment is still in the deal
like finding my way out of Somerville
My imagination is so ill
like coming out of the Gypsy Bar with two white girls
out night walking in South Boston with an ice grill.

A light skinned 70's baby like Redman
who be's for realz
no parents' help
who chose out his honor classes in 8th grade
But still didn't seen every meal
being live from hell
read in 8th grade of Puerto Rican history
on my own interest with the Cuban info
already from popz about us being black there for me
with the allegory
of the darkside
ride in the Buick with the white top and the A track
to the Bearsley Terrace,"little" Robert laid back
with the attention from Ni cee and Connie
with Dumpy and Bubbles in Bldg 10
the chicken, and the lasanga, they made that
I'm now running thru Dorchester less with gas
like running thru dem hallways fast
I blast the best poetry without the trips
across the country like the Harvard's task
the Scroll and Key
My name and family is big like Lowell
and I haven't tackled bodies in the box
like Lawrence
A smooth fox

Can pass rush Alicia Keys in Cape Cod
the water on the rocks
if the girl I'm lalking to now doesn't plot
on me
like this girl Stacy who lived in Quincy
hope she be outgoing like Denise from Brockton
and see the Common
in an adventure here right now
Not passing through Sonora and Fort Stockton
Texas, my state l love also
I remember the alamo
The canoeing in Brighton
like the riverwalk in San Antonio
Been thru Lake Charles, La
Seeing Charles River
the sunset .. a hayday
and clubbing in Fenway
the strip of clubs full of all sorts of women
in the old Factory
and you can win with the Haitians
up in Mattapan
the Avalone be the best play pen
for a single women and men
and I can't wait to eat more of that Puttanesca
in the North End
I'm here for a while
in this world of sin
but out to win
like Paul Revere and the minutemen
But I won't cheer with Samuel Adams
maybe Carlos Rossi
Da me mi mojito my friend
and we can unite
and make things happen
again
stop running like "Whitey" Bulger
We was the first like the opium drug trade beginning
It start right here, man
legal now
No drug sellin
no sin
In the Hub here, the opium
The game started right here
Right here in Boston.

Bridgeport, Da Port Of Envy

What happen to the progress of the youth?
seeing the 3 public high school's image going down
like Father Panik Village, from this city I witness the truth
of shisty politics, police corruption, and the unjust media fabrication.

The nation left this city with its factories of manufacturing
plus Columbia Records and other business too
that started here but not its nothing but the taxing
street action in the 80's and 90's leaving the ground soaked.

and the roots of trees choaked with the blood
and love around is traded for envy
and the hearts of the people is empty to portray the past bitch or thug.
That word bitch is venereal with lust of material

In a city that we witnessed many burials
of murders at a rate much higher than NYC at one point
of victims of circumstance that seen nothing but the imperials
of murder, the projects, especially the Ville
The bricks of 49 buildings had provides loud echoes of drama from your stereo
and Gregory St had to be one of the loudest though yo

Three o ' clock waking up bullet sprays
and you wasn't amazed unless you hear the closest ones
because you know you have one life today
and tomorrow you may see fire that the pastor preaches
and the liquor stores in the cities are like toll booths in this maze
of crack streets of fabricated procrastinating from legalized extortion of taxation
and why the city went bankrupt anyway?

I love the arcades growing up, the confessions I admit
the fact I stoled bikes remember the space invader ones?
and the candy and the money I stoled for it
plus the A & P carriages down that steep street with stray cats
wondering stray bullets off and on, a practice at a tree as that day was lit.

People from New York and some other places got the postcards
of Connecticut
The beautiful homes and the mansions of the rich stars
and the beautiful ride on 95 up the turnpike with the missing tolls

and the souls in the cities you past through in elevation is hard
very hard to image like we should be punished anyway
with the propaganda and the unsigning of ours

The locals but we have no real unity
is this done on purpose?
the envious ones of the community
of a third world city in a wealthiest state,
the definition of America to me?
the concentrated gap of the rich and the poor
demonstrated by those Trendsetters
like the red and the blue pill were sold in stores
but they didn't tell you that the blue wasn't mean't to be yours

Bridgeport, unlike Hartford and Stamford is still fully in the industrial past
well, that explains the prehistoric skyline
where's us, the masses in the equation anyway?
both setting ain't yours or mine
to shout on and knowing me
seeing the value of the dollar decline
like the image of Gun Smoke City throughout the decades
mainly after supporting Adolf Hitler and the past crimes
of wars that Remington Arms and other companies in shadow contracts
that are not found in the Connecticut Post and the New York Times

Shady business
like Vibe Records done to the Skinny Boys
taking money from us too long, yes this I'd witnessed
and show us no love and you got shoves and the hard rug
grounded out in the streets, Connecticut is in the industry's shitlist

Far away, the south got flavor
like fried chicken and sweet yams
15 mins up New England Thruway, and we got no identity that can be major
but the settings like Newark, or Boston and the rest of the Northeast cities
but nothing to say we're real players
but emulating NYC 's talents
and that we all are well off to express hardships with no paper.
Also that is a lie, the industry directed by these people instigated the beef
with our big neighbor.

Bridgeport Da Port Of Envy Part II

As I walk in this world
moving backwards like Michael Jackson
and plus I had a mental surgery
walking in school with 42 kids in the classroom
and half of us is failing
We thinking about what we gonna do after school
so much that we do cut classes
so much we hang out over a friends
playing hookie you call it.
Look at the books that have a signature back to 1950.
when my dad was born
nine years before the Cuban Revolution
When at the school before and during classes
There is a stabbing and a shooting
Guns are quick to get blackmarket
The rejects from Remington Arms
during the whole day somebody sparking it
in the dawn of the dead
from Nuclear warheads
cause my parents ain't taking time to see me about my day
I just spent all of my money I made on rock candy
and Swedish fishes
before I hit with my friends to the Arcade
down two blocks
Plus I snuck out of the house
after my mother had us nap
I taught myself how to ride a bike
That is why I can hitch hike
across the country at ease
and dolo when I go
I open your terrain with plateaus
of street knowledge
So.....
So you can walk on stupid.
Bridgeport ain't no
It ain't no Alpine Texas
It is a jungle for sho
Ya heard
N.O.
No Oasis
A rennasissance here is racist.
Wille is free and done lynched

given us mental face lifts.
smoking a dutch
chasing it
geeked up with the hennie
Many of us dusted
and about to murder mayhem
and dry byes in the 80's and 90's
were like sudden rainfall
then the sun comes out
the words spoken from the so'called harbinger of death
now laughed at
and scorned
because I'm now Job
being afflicted with slanders
That is the thing here in Bridgeport
but before
A fat mouth
was like a snitch
Then the hurse was nursed
In Bridgeport you have prepaid with a Blackberry
and you think you the shit
because you brought some new rims
living in the basement with your moms
and your girlfriend looking for you to answer
When you do
you had agreed in buying her new sneakers
Latinos ain't want to be black
and African American ain't want to be African
They wannabee Spanish and Irish
Damn go to Spain and Ireland
and see if you accepted
and a nigger
you'll get it
Bridgeport is hectic
If you let it
when a hating bum ass nigga
Damn t said it
That nigga wanting to wreck shit
that you posess.
Envious clowns
Like that fed I know from Brooklyn
In the Mosque 7
When I would stretch his ass out in Foster Ave
and expose him in The Van Dyke Houses
When I see my peeps in the South End
I have mad memories

walking with Billy Garrett and my pops
and in the East Side
Kossuth St by St. Charles
walking to My Godfather's house
Coconut Cake
Cape Verdean style
If you got a mob
watch who you beef with
with my fam and connects
and My Cuban temper
to fuck you up.
In Bridgeport we be on that shit
on that envy tip
Cracked out like the crusty bimbos
that be out waiting all day.
When the high class sleep all day
The Cape Verdean and the Brazilian beef
and my brothers speak the same language
The Mexicans here where dusty dead broke
and now some of them women
Chicanos the biggest sellouts
Acting like they don't know Emilano
When yo llego con el preguntando
Some Puerto Ricans here the worst
don't know jack shit about the history
Nuyoricans
Most Afro Americans here can't stand to listen to latin music
Disrespecting the culture
New York ain't show yall love
I told ya
The local artists can't even support each other
The envy
What is with this?
Everybody is a racist
in been segregated.
The slanders and the gossip.
with all this hype tip?
Like this, I'll put it.
So yall get noticed
Represent Bridgeport first
before you represent your click.

New England Underworldz

New England

My home
that we're much misrepresented by the postcards
and history of the Minuteman
My home
where actually its the home of the haters
and sly white politicans
If you don't know about Cape Verdeans
you ain't from here
also about the arcade malls
and Quincy Market
If you don't know about Father Panik
South Providence
Blue Hill Ave
Da Field
Fair Haven
you ain't from here
Like ED OG said, "stop look funny at us."
and you ain't gotta like us
cause if you be at the spot
you will abide by the rules
or your money, car, or you life you lose
Boston hedz pop you quick
and few there tell shit.
if you there in the hood
you know to hit dodge
Hartford hedz pop at you
and their egos' large
Bridgeport hedz was gunsmoke city
home of Remington Arms
now many telling
,but still the Port of Envy
New England hoods East Coast
concrete, smokestacks, factories with gunshells and dead bodies
bums hiding place.
New England Chryme Family, Patriarcia Family, the Cappazillos
Bush Mobb, Da Fountain, Brotherhood, Nation
Latin Kings, Los Solidos, Boriquas Don't Play
La Famila, 20 Love, Humbolt Raiders
street heads with the grey goose
geeked out, buking on to help pay the high cost of rent
annual car tax, property tax here the highest

Home of the Celtics, the Patriots, Huskies, the Suns,
Foxwoods, The original Coves, and the military arms
and haters are nosy sceming trying to befriend you
but envious,
and the girls won't talk
see you in you 2000 Volkswagon, Beamer, or Benz
seduce you with the mission,
You tricking?
Stupid, you weren't listening
Their Additude sickening
No respect of men
Stupid, you still ain't listening
Big name celebrities homes here
I know some
California, the only other place can be
Beverly Hills, and Greenwich, the 60,000 population wealthy town
Big town
and I love Fairfield, Conn, Newton, Mass, and North Providence
plus Cape Cod
with the seafood with wine
the boat off the Massachussetts Bay
Sunset hitting
The way the three family homes look
and way the cold shook
Many shirlens, fur goose, Timbs rocking with the cognac
puerto rican cars, Cape Verdean Social Clubs
Projects ain't condos like the south projects
New England is Northeast baby
Brick living is about that, with Gun powder aroma
asthma, from Smokestack donor
Smokestack to keep on with the oil flue gas
Stupid, you still ain't listening
This is OUR LIFE.
F THE POSTCARDS
F THE MEDIA
F IF YOU DON'T CARE
See you with guns to your throat
with knives against your flesh
By Wild ass Cape Verdeans, Afro-Americans Puerto Ricans, Dominicans,
Portuguese, Brazilians, the italians, like the ones in the Northend of Boston
and some whites here, like the ones from South Boston
F Feminem.
and Hell yeah, The Jamacians are out here with the coco bread
and the weed
Stupid, you still ain't listening
In every Hood from West End Stamford, South End Stamford

Stamford in the 80's was hood.
Remember South kill
You don't know you ain't from Stamford
F if you didn't know
They stuck you for your doe
You acting like yous the only ones on the block
Stupid, you ain't listening
less the shots at you
before that, the guns drawn at you
Fool, the broads will draw on you
South Norwalk,
To New London, small
Misrepresented by that singer from there
Home of the Blacks slaves freed from there
You wasn't listening
Many blood shed
In the 80's, I thought you heard
where you been?
About Bridgeport
Thug Channel
About Money Craven New Haven
You went to Yale and you was afraid to walk to the hood
The Yale police had told you
Now you talking shit
Hating on us
You Bitch
You went to Northeastern and
The Boston Police told you not to go to Jamacia Plain
and Roxbury.
And you heard of the gunshots,
and Read the New Haven Register
and the Boston Globe
and you a bitch talking about us like you a thug
If you are a thug from the hood
you act like you can't get it
because your hood got publicity with rap stars
but your rapstars know
Many of them extorted during or after here
in New England, the most
We're above suspicion
above the map
We know America
America produce us
to be savages in the struggle
while you sitting on your ass
and talking shit about us

But when you walk by us
or come to New England
in the hoods
You froze up.

When the God speaks

When the God speaks
the bellowing bullet frozed
No mantan, no black face
Just a snotty nose
and black socks caught in my heel
Surrounded by Dipilated Factories and smokestacks
as skyscapers over 90 years stand still
seeing older dudes now as old Gs
with ice grills
If not locked up or dead
I saw things in Bridgeport
Many minds got peeled
to the street life
and yield
with the horseman with skulls riding high
Cracked from buking
White lines gave high lies
My mind drifts to see better dayz
like in the suburbs
Soon later it came
But besides seeing or hearing guns spraying
still flames
of the broken homes
for a time
mind blown
Where's a way out?
trom the knowledge of Malcolm
My third eyes minds on
Seeing the big picture
of crack head infested
and court cases
from drugs, murders, diamond necklaces
NO PTA, Promise to Appear
But 25 to 60 years
after raids
and the narks of the remaining two buildings
in the center from eight stories
It played transactions
I was amazed
of seeing the FEDZ
Camera maze
and why the city went bankrupt

Real Estate
and Drug Trade is government runned B
if Connecticut got money
Understanding Connecticut
is understanding America
This shit ain't Funny.

Views of hope to master trials with errors

Liberalism

A key to having freedom of choice
and to display an aurora of expressions
of unconciousness of regrets
and to profound the state of........
The state of what?
What state was the choice of expression ?
When God created the human being
from his image and likeness
Insanity?
Confusion is what Satan said is what this world had begun
Barbaric
Immoral affection
Mr Spock was the victim of Star Wars
after the third of the stars fell from the sky
The State of confusion is profound
the way to take God out of the equation
and the professor was instructed to play professor
with no rules
This is easy
It is easy to be liberal
Free from order
with no concern of future motion
and of the surroundings
It is all about you
Individualism
Why call yourself a mason?
Is a mason liberal?
Do you know?
Freemasonry
Given the right to all human beings naturely
Why the skull and bones?
This game brings about blind confusion illiteracy
Lets stop the motion of thought
and the brain cell is desolate
Cancerous
with no cure
Behavioral patterning

The thinking pattern of the retarded
If you are flagged
there then the rules are played
Liberalism was given for a time
to see if it can work
Take God out the equation
Did this happen before?
Why this happen before?
The dogs came to see their best friend
and the influence is venereal
but not original
The trial in babylon needs no oracle soon You will see no one guiding
and you will see no one motivating
So where is the destination?
Can liberalism add to destiny?
Will it work?

Ojala

That the aurora of the non silent is heard
I wish I can see
a couple in harmony with each others mind
Principle
over
property
Ojala en la tierra
that the married affection
Carino casado
is felt between men and women
I wish I can reach you
and answer every question
and at the beach
at night
looking at the stars of heaven
We can read them
together
Ojala
that we valve
our human lives
and the material things is second
and we are at peace with Zion
and we all are Illuminati
and we illuminate out to the stars
in other galaxies
My DNA can be found on Mars
and outside Galaxy Andromeda
and if I spelled that wrong
May it may not be judged
in hate of my existence
For if the meteor do hit
before I can meet Master Fard
In peace I can lead many to green pastures
in the mind
The mind
The mind
La Oya can be found
if we let laws of nature to coexist
I Will be
Ojala
Let the poor be heard and not be bribed

Let Venezuela be free
Let Cuba be seen as the example of freedom
throughout the world
May finally Africa
All the Cataracts
All of Kemet
be free
All the Pharaohes are human beings
No color is seen
We recognize valve of life
No more wars
Ojala
We all free to produce seeds
and make love
till the day brings the sun
to light our penal glands
and the energy of the ray
It brings our bones to black
the strength of it can bring us back to Memnon
The Temple of Amon is witnessed
May the women rule with the men in affair
May they be look as the GODs they are
Orisha is not a myth
Ojala may I now go to bed to sleep
May China and Russia are looked as human beings
May Babylon cease
No wars
May Russia be true communists
that we see with no optimistism
But optimistism must stay with all thought
So God is present
Ojala
may I now go to bed to sleep
Inshallah.......
I wake up
and make salat
after Wudu
and be brave to to challenge the world
of America
from spiritual laziness
and cowardice.

Trial with errors

Like Vinne Paz said
for most of my life I was torn in two,
If you love me, then this poem is for you
The choice's I make in my life
is sometimes like Job getting more rashy
and the other times not waking up for fajr
will out last me
because in 2 years I misbehaved
acting like Toby blindfolded
being a hell servant like my mother
she neglected my sister
who is slightly handicapped
like a queen bird left a mishap baby in the wilderness

Like the emancipation left us for The Crows
to metaphysically devour what was left
damn why you had to do that?
Now my sister is out like Frida in the streets
without protection, another soup kitchen
and the prisoners of Satan's pill age
grasp her time that is worth nothing
now but the rubble on Samson who let women
in front of his site to see
same to she.....
See you cause her to flee to insanity
and she can't even listen to me
or the rest of the zombies that are kin
that damaged her like now her bad skin
that you try to damage me like
a harbinger of death, stripping me of my underwear
and stoning me with things close to stoning Stephen
like you forge signatures
plus forging my other sister
to not to display her talents
like Frida did without guilt of insanity
with her casado
trying to beat the will out of me
like the wipping of the dying slave
after hardwork and betrayal

just because he or she went to defend their man or womanhood
but you act like George Washington
with no lies
but the mental and physical abuse
were like the 80's drivebys in Stratford Ave
memories like the memories of stray bullets
that wiz and hitting a building
like that crack hitting my father
like lightening though the ceiling
but he never gave me a bad feeling
to almost hate you
out your womb
and I done much to help you
but you do nothing but lead on
like Jezebels trying to ruin Abrahams
and the Fidel would be dead in a godbody
hardly believe, too many will now
when Christanity created by the same,
will be cremated by the same
retardedly believers, too many will bow
so the Sahedrin would feast a great feast of victory
after harvest of Judas
in dead souls
screaming for the mucus of Nebuchchadnezzar to still exist
in his tomb
for like you, the masses were programs to worship pagan images
the hype that lead all of us in the vortex
so the Matrix tricked us to work much
and lose much glory of the covenant in Deuteromony

Human rights you try to topple
But the dream still shines
like armies of Joshua came with the horns
and the dreams of Daniel
the patience of it is like sometimes waiting for fire to stop
the burn the victims of insurance fraud
We're mobbed deep
Like forever burning in hell, I understand
I took the fall, Like Nore said, "Living life in exile"
shun from the Garden of Eden
and the wings were broken
I was scared to read Revelations
I was scared of bad dreams
the fear grew guilt and confession
like lessons of old homicide sessions
My fellow New Yorkers, never dare to think

that the author didn't offered the Pale horse to Bridgeport
like you we daranged and disconnect, plus dangerous
it is the American way
New England ghosts are like crows
with strings with the cup of blasphemy
and rhetoric, gossiping with skull and bone rituals
habitual with sodomizing each
and same with spiritually blowing your brain
and the dying flame
hangs on nooses
using my mom to do this
used to this from the physical bondage
from 1555 reverse the history with number
1619 and you answered the 64 mil
The Manifestation of Losses you will encounter
the forged remissal of the duty
why my mother played in Matthew 24
without the hologram
to perform scrutiny is like Elijah Muhammad with no Malachi of Pluto
Fourth and sixth of the last chapter warning of explosion
4.6 billion miles away, the last platoon
to my knowledge of uncertainty
to understand to complete fate of my mothers explosion of her siblings
to the grave?
The Doors still exists and opened like the walls of closing heaven to grasp
before the Woman shuts her mouth
after she give birth to fruits of Farakhans.

Dwelling on the Omen on our actions

Difficult history

A difficult history it is
such like Silvio Rodriguez said
Sentada sobre el miedo de correr

We sit to run on fear
because of many wars
lost
and we forgotten
we been hinged
closed in
and sold in betrayal
slaverly to a system
of lies and greed
of monopolies of the capitalistic means
and never seeing the dehumanization
and the false representation
Dios
tenias lazos blancos en la piel!!
Sin iglesias
what will you do?
With out the light
in front of you
You are spoiled
with the blanket of the message
you applaud
Why did Pedro Albizu left?
You use the name for fashion?
and you don't seem to know your difficult history
Trapped in Sheol and shallows of hell
Why we chose to be in Egypt
Egypt means bondage
no I'm not an Israelite
Why would yous are proud to be called a child?
Israel is the supplanter
Yous mislead many on that
Why you speak of Christ?
and yous don't practice?
Is material things the principle?
Al Hamdu al Rahman Rabbil al amin

What teacher are you?
If you are afraid to speak
the truth
in behalf of the Minister?
I don't know all the answers
But I know for what I know
of the seed of the tribe of Mannessah, Ephraim , and Judah
Still I know I am not proud of that I WAS an Israelite
To a system of shame and betrayal
I being fed and clothed
and being misinformed
ALL NEWS FITTED TO BE PRINTED
LOOK AT THE TOP LEFT HAND CORNER OF THE TIMES!!!
WE ARE FOOLISH
WE LOOK TO BE DOOMED
But I will not walk with yous
The supplanter will rule for months more
and Bush is not leaving
You think Obama cares?
I'm finished explaining
This land is strange
full of strange people
and they are lost
like herds of cattle
and the Skull and Bones is used to demonize you
and I see bones and no flesh.
Just Skeletor
This land is not of God
and this land trust in evil
with the constitution being use as
a cover for the womb of lies
of Babylon the Great
She is still given birth to devils

Courage to change

The coming of the second time
of the Messiah
when Michael and his angels
will war against the Dragon
this beast
the character warlike
making plans with a nation in desperate need
They dress like worthy men with the mike
posing like they are against evil
with the fight
it is essential
that you get the vibes right
of symbolism and subliminal messages
the hidden light
or of Metaphors Aja Monet's
besides her profound delivery
but the understanding of meaning
take site

It is essential where ever you are
from Brooklyn
or far
in Minneapolis in Paisley Park
to East Los Angeles
in your car
with hydrolics
or If you be in Spain
with a bull ready to spar
and if you be in Cambodia
in the jungles cleaning your scar
Know that it is essential to observe
and be happy of who you actually are

A male or a female
the Feds don't discriminate
on you to be in a cell
and enslavement to debt
and taxs to help them not fail
in paying China back
To you they won't tell
about the reservations that the indians are in
after the TRAIL

is the worst violation of human rights
and the families that was destroyed
in Indonesia and Cambodia
to Thailand and Nepal
To Asia with Hell
like the when the Atomic bomb fell
on Hiroshima and Nagasaki
that Buddha was very dark
and the raping of the Asian women
and the realm of yoga in their minds
in America had fell apart
calling them Poon Tang
the ancient fields of the opium
it is essential that you learn of Asia
Because the land was of all that
Eurasia
Asia Minor
Asia Major
Caucasian
Why mainly asians here cling to them?
But we are naturally asiatic in fact
the Orientals
in the biblical terms
but not to slander with a mocking slap
in the face like the killing of Bruce Lee
the plot
you see
what revolution was that he
that he brung in styles
with no name

Like the truth
has none
but the wicked
hid it in pieces and gave them some
like adding on and taking away
supplanting was done
to the ancient prophets
to leave doubt
to it you are strunged
from circumstances
and you was brung
to believe even that of Michael Jackson
had tongued
down children
and that the Black Panthers

had just invaded the White house building
you now wishing
on a change
times before, a million
from a single person now
that was endorsed by wicked beasts with no feelings
but to set up a World Union
to enslave humanity
and many killings
if you out to protest in the future
it is essential that you educate yourself
to conduct yourself now
so they fail in enslaving your soul
how?
Shall you stay a robot
living foul?
and working yourself to death
My fellow Mexican people walking for miles
but not being a Zapatista
To protect the child of you mestiza?
To my latinos
What is so wrong in being a comunista?
Should we stay divided
and anti social
the envy and the hate
to go postal
we need to build
to ourselves in our humanity we must get vocal
to our families
and my Afro Americans
why stay think we a part of America
when we are considered 3/5ths
and we continue to sit and watch
and when we are insulted
we riot and go sick
and we lose again
of not controling our emotions and not organizing
it is essential
That self education
of the Nation tha is still rising
and self doing to be on the horizon.

Wrath of the Math

Like Jeru, here comes the wrath
like the Ancient of Days
the people ain't ready, so it is like a plague
and they aren't people, they are vampires
trangressor in every shape, color and form.
Word is born in the scriptures of them in codes
and behold the horse man with the white mare
and blood in his cup,
drinking it like tea and laughing
plus the vampires cheering him on the prowl
and fight against the ones firm on foundations
of the fountain that gives pro verbs and
you must study the secrets of Daniel
Yes I am Nathaniel
and Oriyama'at is the struggle
and to find it,
It appeared in numbers before
and I saw the vision of the vampire
when I first saw her eyes again
I care not to bother
and act like I never known
Things is painful to see
but numbness to the game you must be.
emotions and patience
is like blood and water
pouring on your back when you are sleep walking
and talking baal
like a witch, when she said my 2000 volkswagon Golf was given
and not worked for
A witch she may not be, but the set had slipped in
for a moment. For the time beening I don't know
But that the fact that the set can slip up in me too.
but the sentence with the question remained reluctant
with the intent to give me acknowledge and respect
that I am a hard working and self liberated man
and setbacks
was a gift, like Jacob was to planning the world in chaos
but the entire mission was to enimently purify
and some that was made became
and took kind out of man
and some ate with the elders

and bore fruit
The fruit was made to last and cycle another 25,000 years
and so
from the clot, that is 96
To make a nation takes age and not color
but think first before you act
and you might understand this
and not, like Redman said, laugh now
and press rewind, Poverty's Paradise
and Hell on Earth, are congruent
Are we Naughty by Nature?
This world will go round in flames
Nay you unbelievers of the word
mock me for what I just wrote
that is murder and you will get the wrath
and the math is deeper than the Kemetian/Mayan Calendar
keep playing with your time
and we in the Third woe
that the dragon with that horn
the so 'called unicorn's father had drawn in his mind.
maybe you didn't see the book yet with his appearence
You was distracted by the lynching
talking about freeing willie again.
It was freed already and there is only 5 years left.

Wake from Bilal

They bless to Bilal
and they walk with arrogance of Judas
with their mortal flesh
and they keep making blasphemy
against the threshold of Judah
and against the covenant that was given
to despair the yoke
after 1934, the sacred secret was revealed
and since few studied.
The star and the crescent
takes shape of the earth
after 1914, the collapsing of the grip of Satan
and the coming of Abraham
and the faith of prophets of every nation
to yearn for the past of faith of men
and the unity of all to be as human beings
as one
and not as savages
for the Great Mahdi was sent forth
and was given to mark death of the womb
the cave of the enemies
who betray with advancement of slanders
the mountains shall fall
there is no hiding placing
From Judah came out a warner
before the great destruction
you must come out of her
and you families of past tribes
been taught to hate the covenant
for now you are scattered
for you let the wicked deceive you
and you now want to stay with the mark
You are foolish to think Bush will leave
and you are foolish to submit to the system
that make you shame of your true self
and likeness to be the khalifah
The Ka' bah is the sign to not forget
but some of you worship it
You criticize me to say these words
and you aught for once

to shut up and listen
and stop the traditions
for the Nebuchadnezzar has risen
the King Herod has risen
The Beast with the small horn has risen
Study symbolism
Stop the slander
The Beast with the Ten horns and Seven Heads is wrathful
and the Ancient of Days are here
Just look of the hate crimes
Soon back to lynchings
You rebellious people
you are deserving of this
Yes I am a mortal
and like Ponitus Polite
I see no wrong in Christ
You take the title to fashion
and cover your lying life
and some of you lay down with the same sex
Rebuking Leviticus
Rebuking the Old Testament
and slandering the ones who are purifying.
Like Ponitus Polite
after the water and the blood
I see no death
But yous are so blind
You think the second coming is dead
You think the second coming is a myth
You think the second coming had not come
You foolish savages
He came and is here
Armaggedeon is now
Reverse the numbers
Now the women are judged
for they are the sign of the temper of the nation
for they been betray and been brought down
to be Jezebels
and wicked in coniving
and they learned from the false polygamists
For the sunnat is for the annointed
But yous made to believe all the prophets had sinned
So you slander
and you behave in the acting
but a slave you are
and by the way you act
you think you and the Beast are power

Like Master Fard is not in the mist
to your doom.
Coming out of her
and Yes, the demon crats
Democratis
You been made to be illiterate.
Study the number 19.

The struggle of my humanity

My humanity.....you despise me.

Can't you grow up?
You acting with Jimmy Swaggert
You still didn't get it?
Why do you still persist
that I'm going to fall for the BS?
Why do you still call me and I don't answer?
I told you earlier that I fell asleep and later in 30 min
I'll come and pick you up.
But I didn't
You still calling, and I don't answer
Why do you come to me asking how I got the place?
Why do you act all friendly?
Why do you think a young black man as myself can't get a nice place?
and I can't cook now?
I didn't ask to be put in a box.
because I don't subjugate myself, I'm out to be free
Free like Martin Luther said in his last speech
and I don't need to shake a white man's hand
or yours to be free.
I speak of human rights too.
Now I'm an angry black man.
But no brown or black man or woman has gone to the white house
to throw a bottle.
Yeah, I saw the indian figure on the top.
I just swallow my pride and let the BS ride
Qtip of the Tribe said the same thing
All this BS is trial, but temporary.
Yes, I have an ego
I should feel good about myself
and I don't trip.
and you don't need to send me messages
I just showed common courtesy
That is my mannerism
One thing about me, is that I don't stereotype
Pero, no creo en nadie ya.
Now I'm too Black to be Cuban?
Ochun, efa , taboo , taboo.
I'm too light

and suppose to be ignorant and stupid to know that I'm african.
But the dance, the food, and no matter how light we are....
we African
So stop the lies.
But you people around me the worse.
Yea, I'm not perfect by the long shot
and so are you.
Stop the 5 deadly
and come down from the ladder
Because you don't have the affiliation with the supplanter

I'm not suppose to ask you out?
But you suppose to take my money?
You want to drive my car?
I'm not suppose to have a nice car either?
I'm suppose to be what you think of me.
and thats that.
You want to say now that I'm crazy?
Now I can't stand up for myself.
Because I suppose to be slow and stupid
Because I have bashfulness and passion
I suppose to be content with savagery
My manhood is gone with the Patriot Act
I'm a animal?
I'm still going to speak the truth and stand up
No patriot act
HELL NO!
None of yall trangressors in the masses going to get the best of me.
At first you ain't suppose to trust no one in this life anyway
Respect must be like a raise
Earned
Yes, I'm from Connecticut
and proud of it too.
Yes I'm a follower of Farakhan

Now I'm suppose to hate white people?
Don't say that I ain't a muslim
Yes my last name is Oriyama'at
A made up name
and yes a female corrected me to properly pronounce it
and yes I legalized it after.
Because that is my human right
I'm not with the program to be americanized
I speak english, but I'm not english
I speak spanish, but I'm not spanish
I don't know shit about the Cuban Revolution?
lol......You got alot to say.

Some of yous think alot to say bad about me.
Yes I have a passion for Yoruba
That is my culture
Now some of us is too light to speak yoruba?
Egyptians weren't black?
Timbuktu was a black libary
Are africans really jungle monkeys?
and we practice voodoo?
What is yoga then?
You raped us and our lands
F the Media
I hardly watch TV
Hell with your lies.
What is a Zionist
What is the proper definition?
and yes I'm a Jew
No I'm not confused
Are you?
Hum....
What more are you saying about me?

Words of Concern of the Nation

Last Of A Dying Breed

The last of a dying breed
to this I can't believe
I was spoiled with a litl patience
when I was a youn G
Don't get it twisted
I mean G.O.D
naturely given the key
but in this fucked world
it wasn't be
In a city where the good die young
in three dimensions B
It seem that all three was gone
But the Father was with me
Yeah, I was a product of BPT
Gun Smoke City
Don't get it twisted
It ain't just where the gunz were made
But where the gunz were sprayed
In the 80's
plus 90's
many bodies were layed
but the mind gets delayed
to be a human being
when you ain't taught to display
like the Honorable Elijah Muhammad had said
already you stealing from your mother in the Ist grade
and seeing the broking glass in the streets by the cars
even give you more ideas
Because you been brought in the iniquity
of a broken home
At first like me
of a Drug/alcoholic man and a materalistic mommy
the last of a dying breed
from the Constitiution state
they call it CT
where in BPT I see the old BPT police cars
locking up headz getting felonies
of drugs and murders
and the Party is not over
of extortions and

frauds in my life
but through it all
I chose not to become trife
and lead myself to become worthy
and out of situations thats tight
at the same time, in phases
The father was giving me the light
about this no good chickenheads
the backstabbing family
and envious cats that ain't right
with their ways
they minds died young in these streets
beening stressed out
and the money means nothing
when yourself is surrounded by fiends
of all sorts
The Party is stll not over
even though the murder rate is way down
but they ain't putting out much info clown
but the courts is still filled up downtown
just telling you straight
that they ain't playing around
Were the last of the dying breed
no matter the way you look at it
You need to believe
We lost the family unit too
Willy Lynch 1712-2012
The Party's ain't Over
Can't you see?

Quiere me como soy

Quiere me como soy
porque no intimidacion de otros
es un falta de nosotros
Como la lluvia se venga
Se caer
Eso de mi pecho malo cuando estoy enojo
No mojo
Pero solo cuando antisocial,
Cuando no quiere hacer nada
porque del tiempo afuera
que atacar mi pecho
No siempre en el derecho
porque mi circumstancia es muy progressive
contra poder mio

Quiere me como soy
cuando hablo sobre mi madre
Quiere me negado
y yo no tiene mucho familia
que no visito
y tambien no lleva con pecho aristocratico
Quiere me como soy
cuando no tiene la mula pa' pagar pa' un vola
Cuando preguntas que tu quieres a mover mi 2000 volks
Diriate no.
que mi espanol y ingles es no mejor
Cuando no mas gusto cuando llego a casa
Cuando cuego mi a besarte porque
tus mentiras estoy llenado de mierda
y diga te que necesitas a quedar de tus amigas
cuando ellas dicen chismes.

Quiere me como yo
Si, hablo contra los politicos
y quiere a representar Africa y Cuba total
es mi cultura
Es que soy
Soy mestizo
y como mezcla
mi estilo es mas differente
Yo represento mi gente
Tu tambien como eres
Todo sobre que tu eres

como eso quiere me
Mis faltas, quedar conmigo
porque manana yo se ganare'
Mi agenda es pa' ganar
Cuando yo piedo
quiere me
Porque cuando yo gano sigiente vez
La victoria sera paraiso.

Love in the end

Re.......Wind

Re...... wind

Should I look back?
was her name Sarah with Lot
or Sheba?
The Queen with a conscience
that gravitifies all matter that exists
to listen
The voice sounds like the violin
by Geronimo Pratt playings
and with fire like Emilio Zapata's eyes
She was new to me like Silvio Rodriguez
by suprise with revolutionary cadenas
of Souljourner Truth
kicking the nigger out of your mind
so you and say.....God
Her voice had sent The Nile through my spine
and like hip hop.....my head nod
because her voice was seducing to me
like she knew my thoughts and
repeated.....with a female tone
and I was jumping.....like a candy store robbery
all of the sweets under my pillow
and I was sucking with a grin
Her thoughts sounded kin
with the flow of nile through my arteries of emotions
that triggered attention
like a Satellite dish
She was on radar
and I was the CIA
Curiousity In Action
after the neglect and resistance of Bridgeport tramps
that are like sugar in Kool Aid
too much.
Too much chaos
and Why I feel like a merciful Judge

when I slammed the hammer twice on her
with doubt
Curse God and die?
to say that he can't grant me a companion
to be Mary and I am Abraham
with fire of a lamb
to come to her once again to feel lost
In front of people in silence.... when she rejects.....
again?
Abraham to his throne
Ham is no curse; the rhetoric was shown
between two brown noses with smelling
hot stenchs of bablyon
and the cup with blood stains
she may seems to know that I don't carry it
nor I take part of drinking the blood
in my thoughts.....
nor the sweat....
For I want the proper things
because I can't even resist
forgettabbouttit
Her mind looks like a gallery of the word "Imhotep"
and call for shades
to cover my eyes to hinder
my thoughts
that seems to look like lunacy to many
But she may understand me
congruency
She is too vocal to resist
my temptation is like waning to see Cuba
Haram is not likely
to see that I can't fish for the hands reaching......
into the Ark
of the covenant that she speaks on the soul
to reach in The Book
that the devil will be cast out forever by thought
and we may never be aggressors in spirit together?
to build....and to cancel out the immorality
and the humanity together is like Rollingstones
at The Doors to rage against the machine of iniquity?
Maybe I am crazy.
like Jesus....I should chill and smoke and drink again
and won't see heaven at the footsteps,
because I am no muslim with no Maryam
and the Manifestation of Losses was like....
The tap water I can only drink in offices

why I can't drink in times normal
when I suppose to drink.
The cup is new and ready
Soddam and Gommorahh repeats
But at her presence
I press re.....wind.

with no regrets.

My Favorite Poets
- Jose Marti
- Langston Hughes
- Oveous Maximus
- Aja Monet
- Camilo Palmeri
- Sonia Sanchez

The Books that had influenced me
- Autobiography of Malcolm X
- Old Man and the Sea
- The Bible
- The Quran
- Message to the Black Man
- Payback is a Bitch, by Marcus Spears
- Ernesto Che Guevara....I read two books on him
- Fidel Castro......I read four and a half books on him
- 40 Cuban Revolution Reader
- Sun Tzu - The Art of War
- Choosing the Gap- By the Minister Farakhan
- Shades of Memnon Part I

The movies that had influenced me
- Distinguished Gentleman
- Do the Right Thing
- Malcolm X
- Scarface
- The Godfather movies
- Bronx Tale
- City of the Gods
- The Matrix
- Hellspawn

The TV shows
- The Cosby Show
- A Different World
- Fresh Prince of Bel Air

New York Undercover
Yo MTV Raps/Rap City
Caribbean Rhythms

My favorite music that had inspired me
Prince
Michael Jackson
A tribe called Quest
X-Clan
The Guru
Tupac Shakur
Rakim
Redman
Wu Tang Clan(Every last one of the members)
Christopher Williams
The Isley Brothers
El General
Eddie Santiago
Orishas
Tego Calderon
Silvio Rodriguez
Compay Segundo
Omara Portunondo
Ibrahim Ferrer
Celia Cruz
Jedi Mind Tricks
The Roots
Nas(He's one of the best)
Lauryn Hill
Scarface
Ras Kass
Common Sense
Bob Marley
Capelton
Super Cat

Favorite Sports People that had inspired me
Kareem Abdul Jabbar
Magic Johnson
Mike Singletary
Walter Payton

Rodney Harrison
Tom Brady
Ty Law
Danny Tartabull
Roberto Clemente
Mike Tyson
Wade Boggs

AUTOBIOGRAPHY

Robert Oriyama'at (born in Bridgeport, CT), is a United States Airforce veteran, who takes pride in making a difference in people's lives. In Bridgeport growing up. He said "You used to seeing people with the burner on them." "Bridgeport wasn't a place you would just mouth off without a burner on you." "Especially if you was from out of town." That is not what he wanted to be influenced by. He had already knew that some of the people in the streets where good people but they were brought up in the bad circumstances of poverty. That is the reason Robert had went in the Military. The military was a safe haven for Robert. He started to learn more of his Afro-Cuban, Native American and Afro American roots thru study. He started to listen to more latin music. "Thanks for the influence of Mexico in where I was just from the border in Laughlin, AFB, Texas. in a town of Del Rio. His spanish started to get much better at this time because. of the influence of being in Mexico. So when he spoke it.There was little problem. He had made a surprise encounterment with the Zapatistas in Piedras Negras Zapatistas is known in Piedras Negras(BlackRock) big time.Where in Bridgeport in the Black Rock section, an affluent section of Bridgeport. Many Mexicans live there and many Mexican businesses are there. Robert has been to New Orleans, Alabama, Mississippi, Oklahoma, Seattle, Chicago, Korea, etc.In 2001, he left the U.S Airforce for good. He has the upmost respect for the military. But he sees that the U.S. government at the time was mislead the armed forces. He left as a "conscientious objector." At the same time he had enlisted in the Nation of Islam.Everywhere he went he repped Bridgeport and New England. He now resides in Boston in the Dorchester section of town. Boston is like a mini New York. Boston has its own Boroughs. There are good large cities bordering Boston, like Somerville, Cambridge, and Quincy.etc. "Many people outside New England have a misunderstanding of New England" he states. "That the media makes half truths of many things." Robert has been writing since he was 15. He started rapping and writing actual rhymes of his own since he was 17. He was in a couple of groups in the Military. He states that he met a Mexican named Q VO from East L.A. who was a music producer. "One of the coolest dudes I met. Very down to earth...""He wanted me to be part of what he was doing." "He was becoming a producer." "I started to record with him." "It was also this guy from Danville, Virginia. I now can't recall his name, but he was with us as well." "We all recorded together." By time Robert had went to Korea. He started to record himself and he had sent some copies to the Gangstarr Foundation, The Wutang Clan, and The Def squad.."But I didn't have any original beats." "Or studio equipment....But, I constantly worked on my flow." By the time he met with Khemraf in 2003. He started to record again and made two songs. Both was freestyle that he had recorded. But one stood out called "Absolute Conscience". Khemraf had produced the beat and his cousin Kemet and him started to record. He is currently working with Khemraf. When he first went to the Nuyorican Cafe. In which he said he finally went.In 2006, he met a girl who had influenced him to take poetry seriously. Her name is Aja Monet, an Afro Cuban/AfroJamacian self defined poet in New York...He noticed the similarity of his thoughts,and writings with hers."I was embraced with her influence." He didn't connect with Aja. But he went on to write poetry again. He started writing poetry in 2002. He made works for Providence, Rhode Island at a church where they had a cafe in the basement.He was persuade to go there by a girl name Tanisha, a Cape Verdean church goer and a student of the bible. He had met her with his cousin Kemet at the Cape Verdean parade in Indian Point, Providence, Rhode Island. The second poetry was a controversal one that he had done for a talent show in Muhammad's Mosque # 7. He was questioned by a phrase that he had said about the government, in which he had nararated of the voices of people who are criticizing the government. Still today he is becoming one of the anchors of poetry.

www.ingramcontent.com/pod-product-compliance
Lightning Source LLC
Chambersburg PA
CBHW051713040426
42446CB00008B/868